Benoit Tardif

METROPOLIS

B P P

MONTREAL

👤 4 million　　💬 French / English　　🏴 Canada

Notre-Dame Basilica

bagel stand

BAGEL SHOP

HOT BAGELS — OVEN BAKED

Clock Tower (45m)

ice hockey player

6

AAAAAAH

theme park

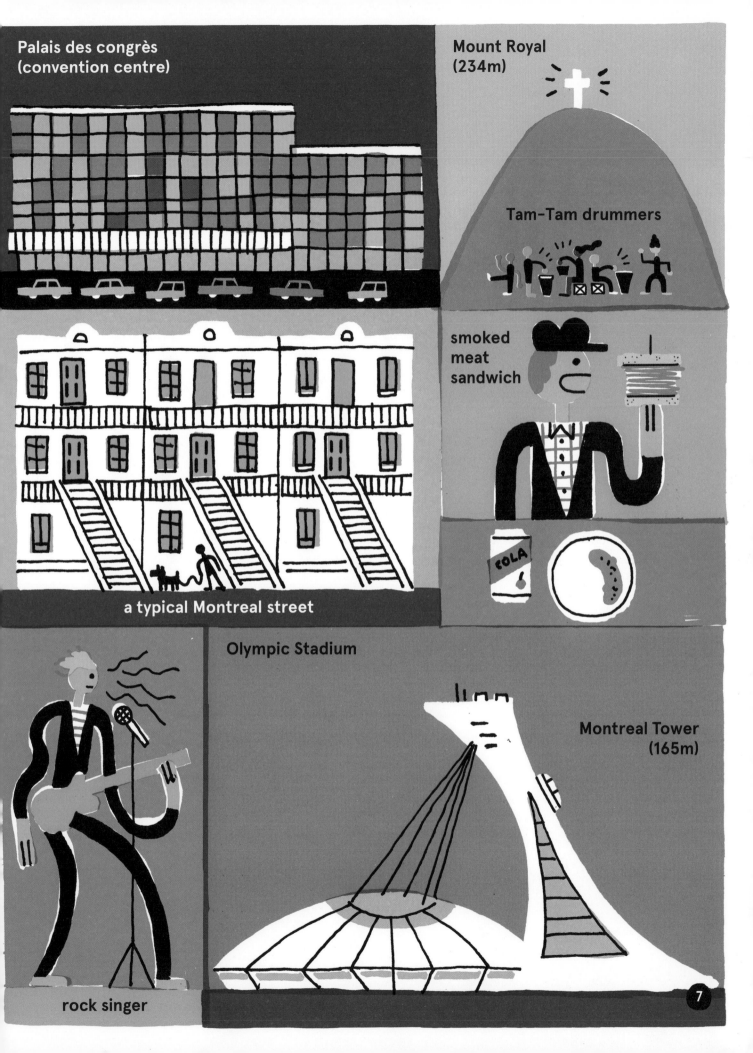

Palais des congrès (convention centre)

Mount Royal (234m)

Tam-Tam drummers

smoked meat sandwich

a typical Montreal street

Olympic Stadium

Montreal Tower (165m)

rock singer

7

TORONTO

👤 6 million 💬 English / French 🚩 Canada

blue jay

CN Tower (553m)

Stanley Cup in the Hockey Hall of Fame

Royal Canadian Mounted Police

walk on the waterfront

Rogers Centre (sports stadium)

Lake Ontario

8

City Hall

GO!GO!GO!

ice hockey player

ice rink

doughnut stand

Royal Ontario Museum
(natural history)

NEW YORK

 23.6 million  English United States of America

Chrysler
Building
(319m)

baseball
player

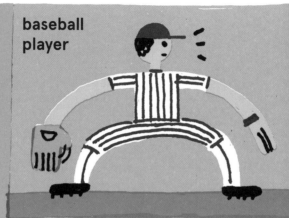

HOT DOGS

hot dog stand

Guggenheim Museum

traffic on 42nd Street

10

yellow taxi

New Yorkers in a hurry

TAXI!

TAXI!

New York-style bagel

I ♥ NY

I love NY t-shirt

Statue of Liberty

river cruise

Central Park

New York diner

DINER

subway

stories tell of alligators living in the sewers

11

CHICAGO

👤 10 million   💬 English   🏴 United States of America

Buckingham Fountain

blues musician

Marina City Towers (179m)

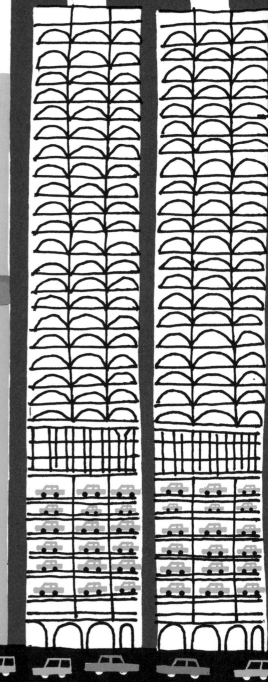

The Wrigley Building

cruise on the Chicago river

Willis Tower (442m)

Michigan Lake beach

Cloud Gate sculpture

Chicago Dog (beef hot dog with pickles and chilli)

baseball player

THE FANS LOVE ME!

elevated train

SAN FRANCISCO

 8.6 million 💬 English 🏴 United States of America

Golden Gate Bridge

San Francisco Bay

Coit Tower (64m)

Russian Hill area

sea lions at Pier 39

cioppino (seafood stew)

14

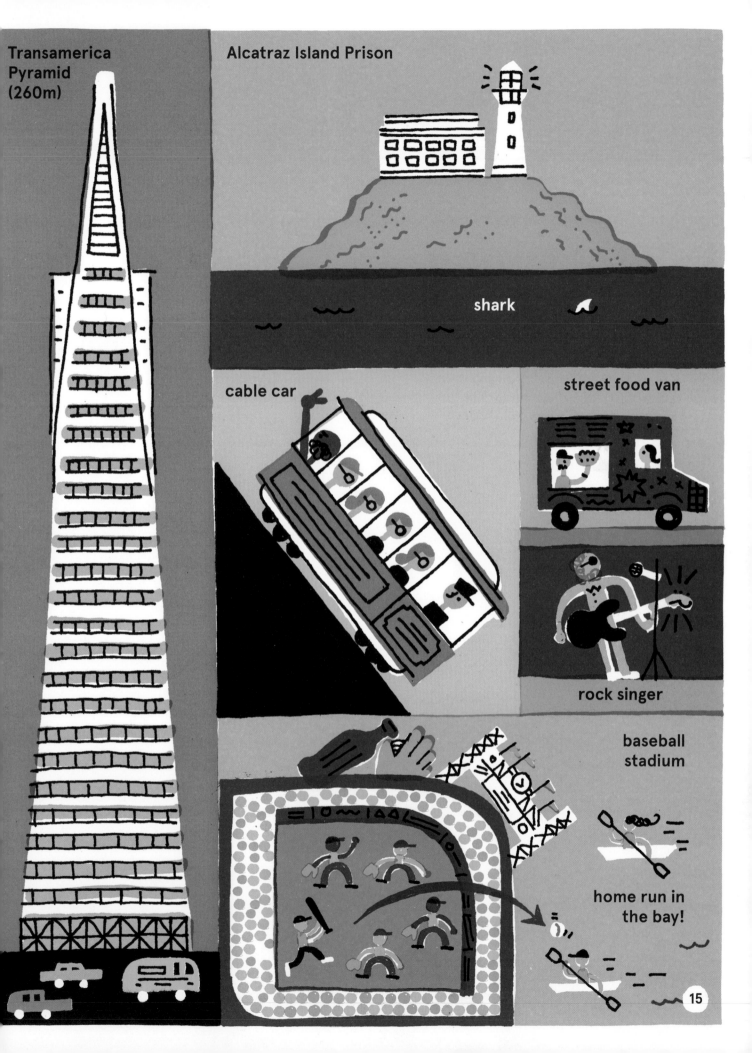

MEXICO CITY

👤 20 million 💬 Spanish 🏳 Mexico

Mexico City
Metropolitan
Cathedral

Paseo de la
Reforma
(main avenue)

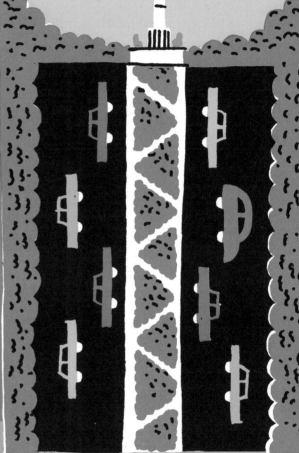

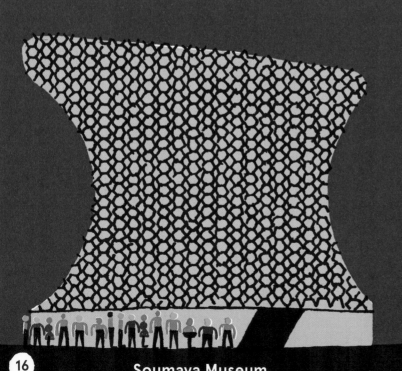

Soumaya Museum

pambazos
(sandwich
filled with
chorizo
and potato)

green taxi

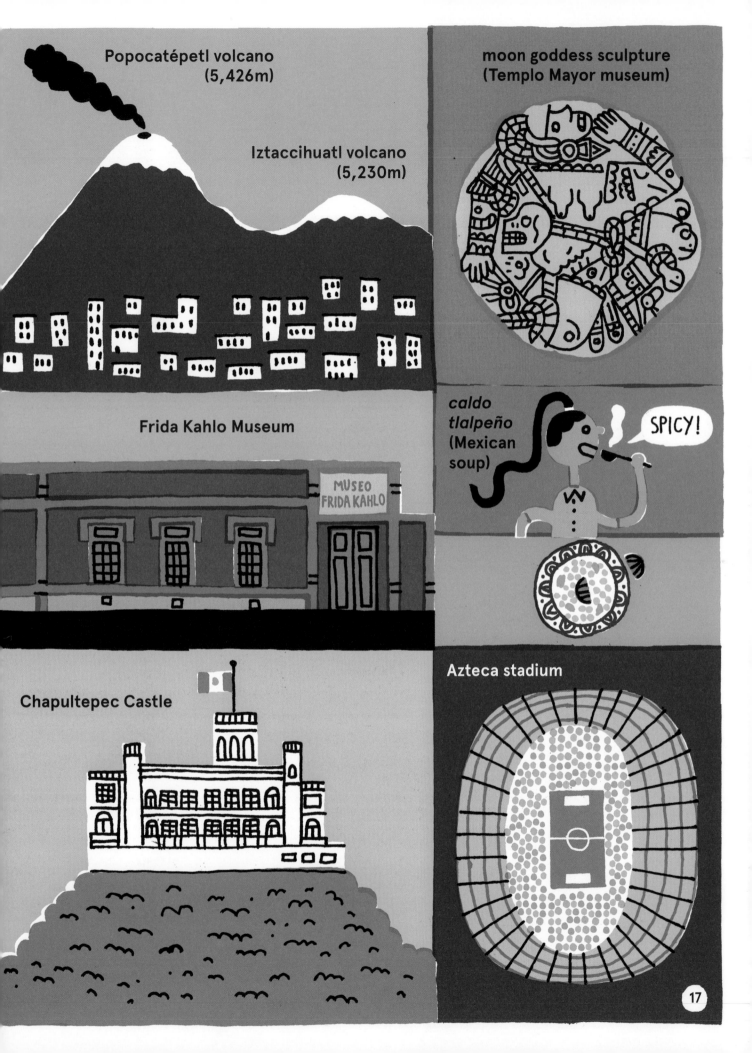

Popocatépetl volcano
(5,426m)

Iztaccihuatl volcano
(5,230m)

moon goddess sculpture
(Templo Mayor museum)

Frida Kahlo Museum

MUSEO FRIDA KAHLO

caldo tlalpeño (Mexican soup)

SPICY!

Chapultepec Castle

Azteca stadium

17

RIO DE JANEIRO

👤 12 million 💬 Portuguese 🏴 Brazil

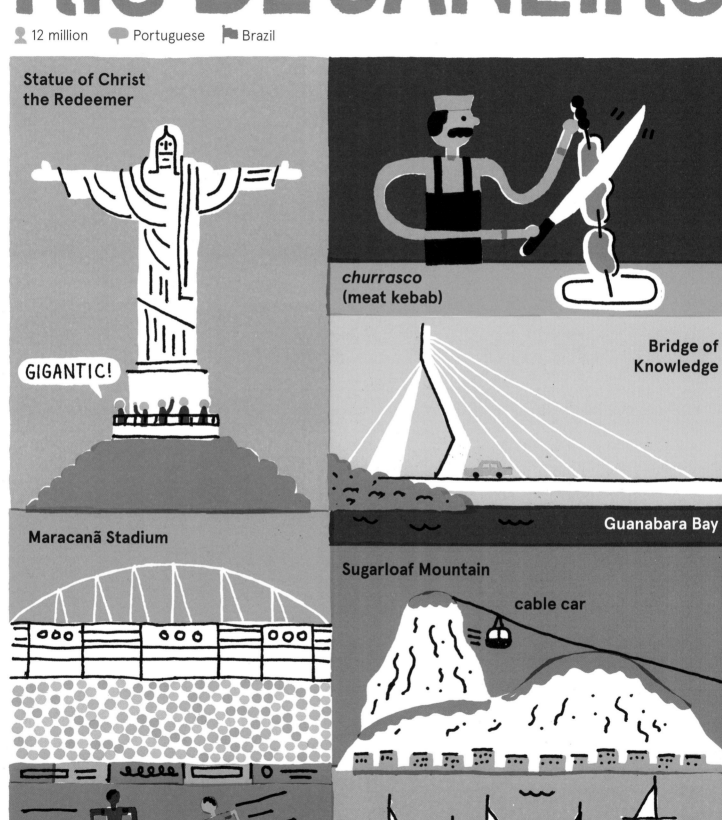

Statue of Christ the Redeemer

GIGANTIC!

churrasco **(meat kebab)**

Bridge of Knowledge

Guanabara Bay

Maracanã Stadium

Sugarloaf Mountain

cable car

BUENOS AIRES

👤 14 million 💬 Spanish 🏳️ Argentina

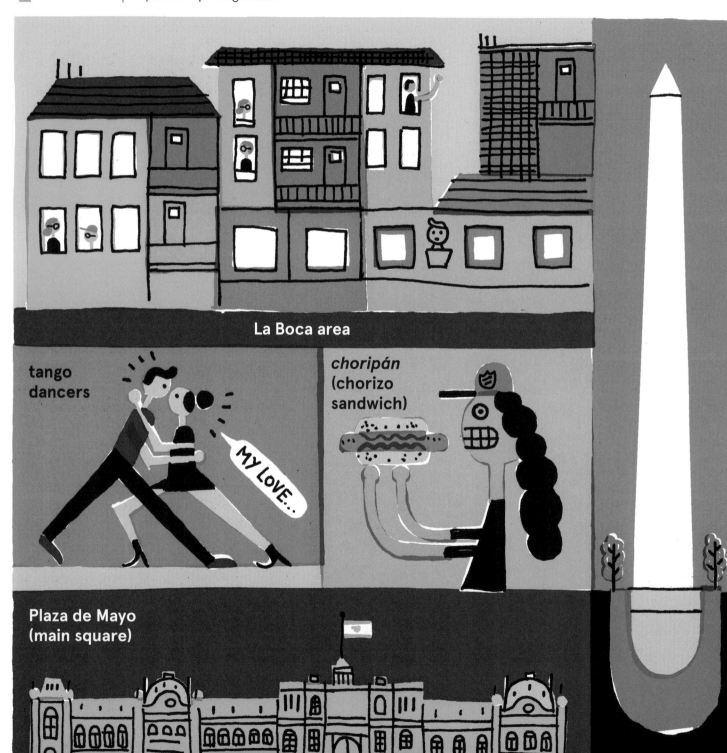

La Boca area

tango dancers

choripán (chorizo sandwich)

My love...

Plaza de Mayo (main square)

Obelisk of Buenos Aires (68m)

20

monuments at La Recoleta Cemetery

Colón Theatre

Floralis Genérica Sculpture

football player

Buenos Aires Zoo

Puente de la Mujer (rotating footbridge)

Puerto Madero waterfront

LONDON

 13.7 million 💬 English 🏴 United Kingdom

telephone box

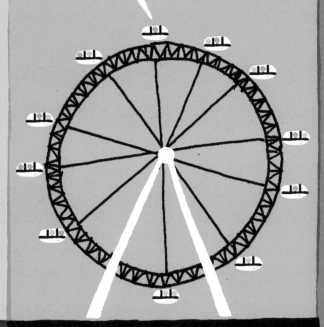

London Eye

(22) **tube sign**

double-decker bus

30 St Mary Axe skyscraper (180m)

'The Gherkin'

PARIS

 12.3 million  French 🏳 France

newspaper kiosk

gendarme (police officer)

French baguette

Arc De Triomphe

Eiffel Tower (324m)

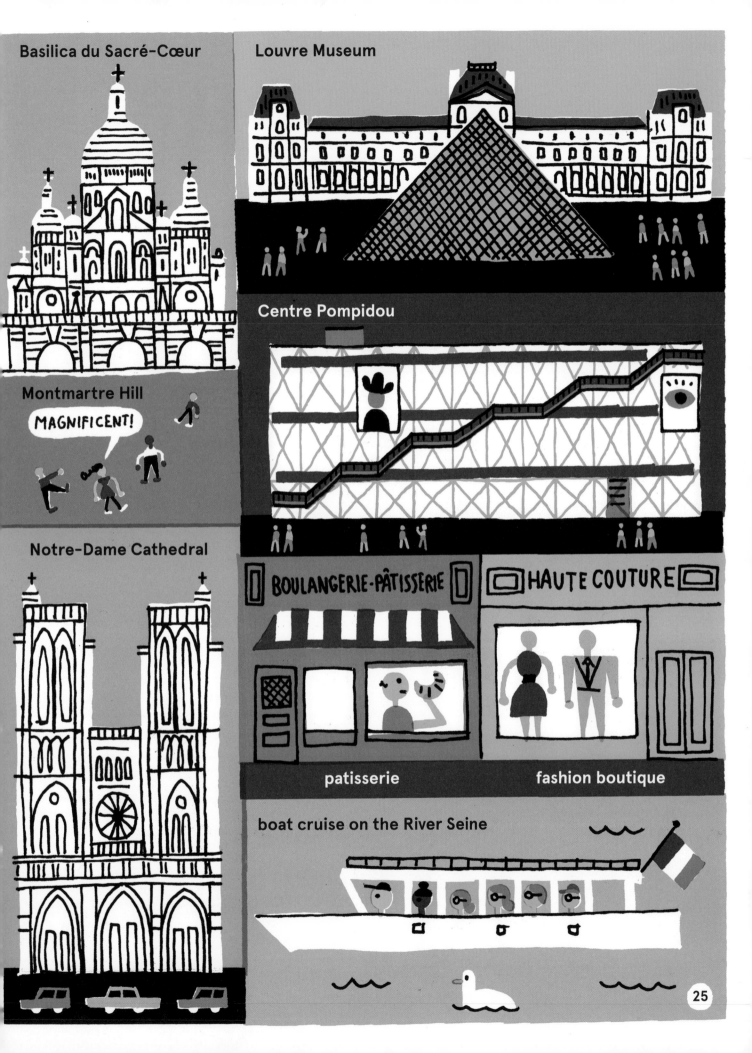

AMSTERDAM

tulip

👤 2.3 million 💬 Dutch 🏳 Netherlands

Amsterdam Centraal Station

windmill brewery

cyclists along the canals

canal

stroopwafel
(syrup waffle)

26

row of townhouses

Rembrandt, Van Gogh and Vermeer
paintings at the Rijksmuseum

bike taxi

TO VONDELPARK, PLEASE!

football
player

patat
oorlog

(fries,
mayonnaise,
peanut sauce
and onions)

flower market

ZURICH

 1.3 million ● German ⚑ Switzerland

Zurich Opera House

Grossmünster church

Uetliberg Mountain (871m)

Uto Kulm Hotel

swimming in the Limmat river

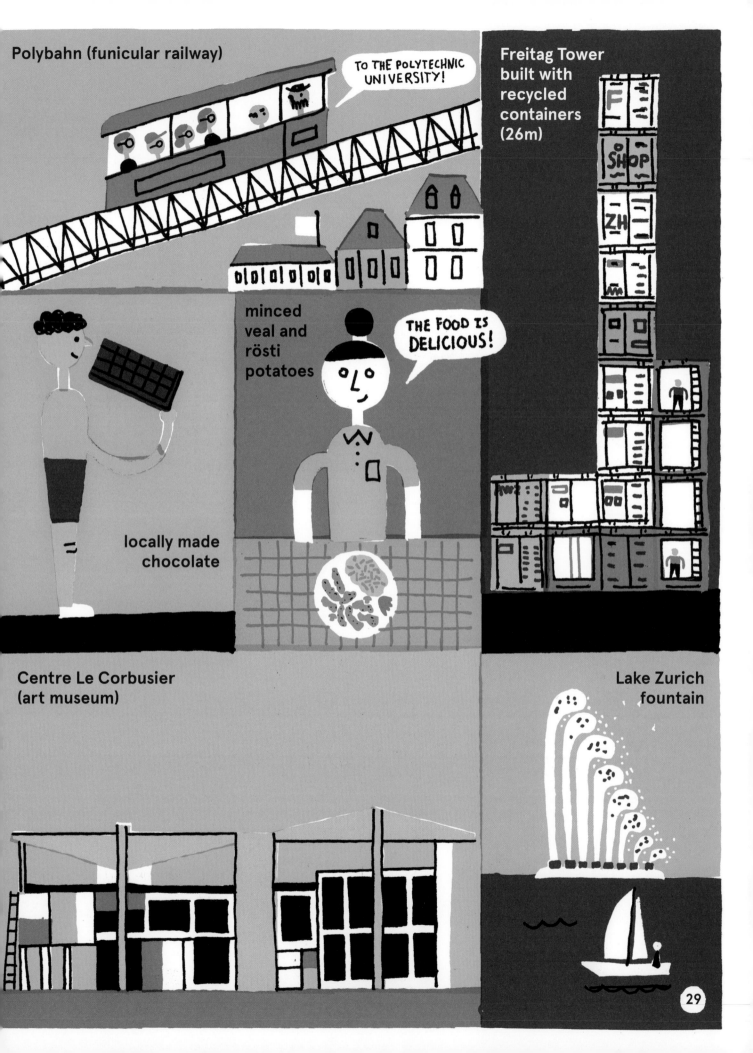

BERLIN

👤 4.4 million   💬 German   🏳️ Germany

döner kebab

TV Tower

Reichstag Palace
(German parliament building)

painted bear sculptures

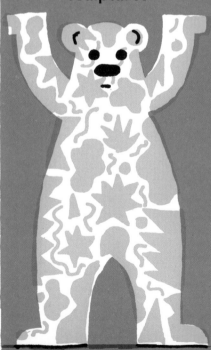

the symbol
of Berlin

Brandenburg Gate

Fernsehturm
(368m)

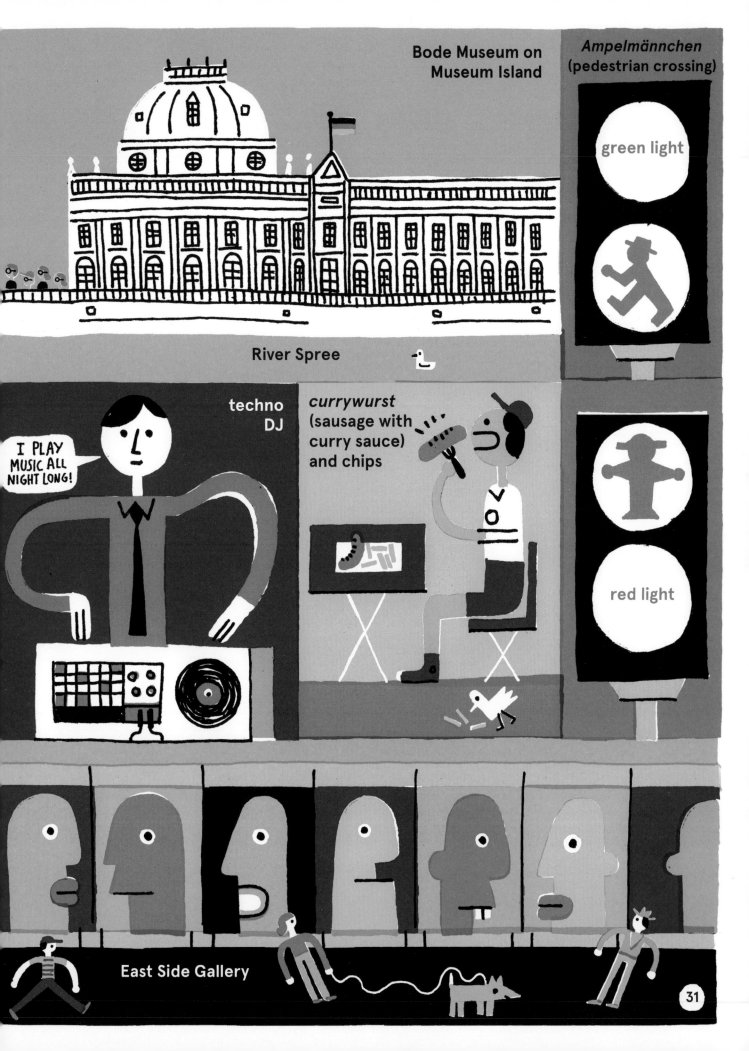

KRAKÓW

 1.5 million   Polish   Poland

Kraków Cloth Hall

Saint Mary's Basilica

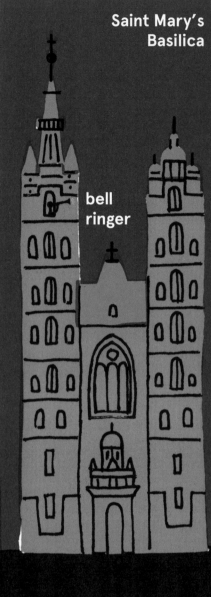

bell ringer

St. Florian's Gate

sightseeing by golf cart

jazz concert

obwarzanek (bread plait)

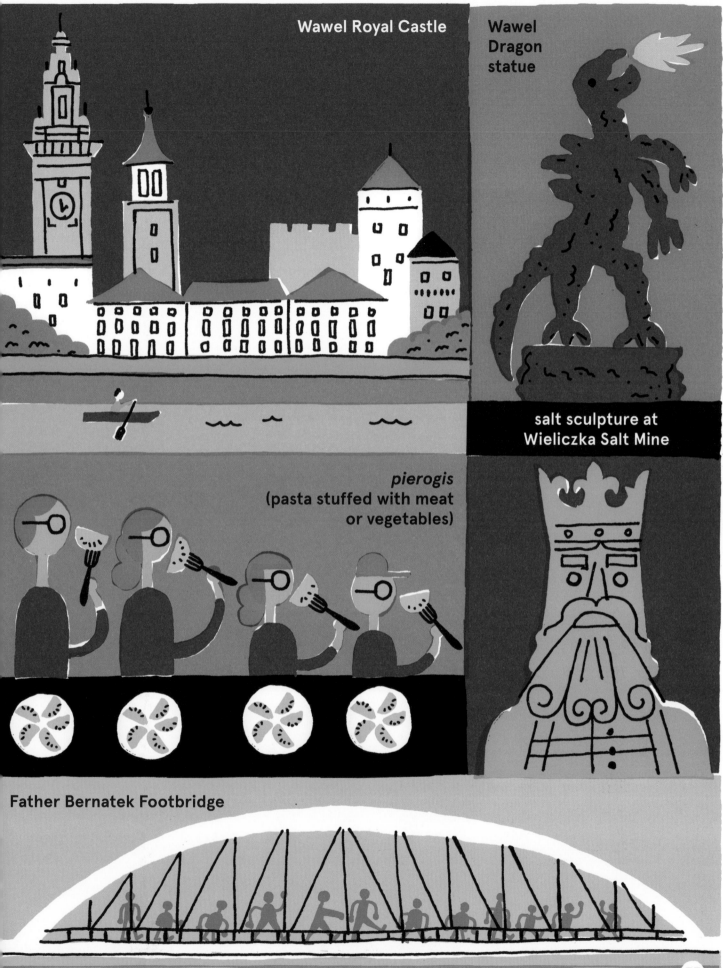

Wawel Royal Castle

Wawel Dragon statue

salt sculpture at Wieliczka Salt Mine

pierogis (pasta stuffed with meat or vegetables)

Father Bernatek Footbridge

Vistula River

STOCKHOLM

👤 2.2 million 💬 Swedish 🏳 Sweden

Pippi Longstocking

Royal Palace

Norrström (waterway)

City Hall

Lake Mälaren

Royal Palace Guard

kanelbulle (cinnamon roll)

34

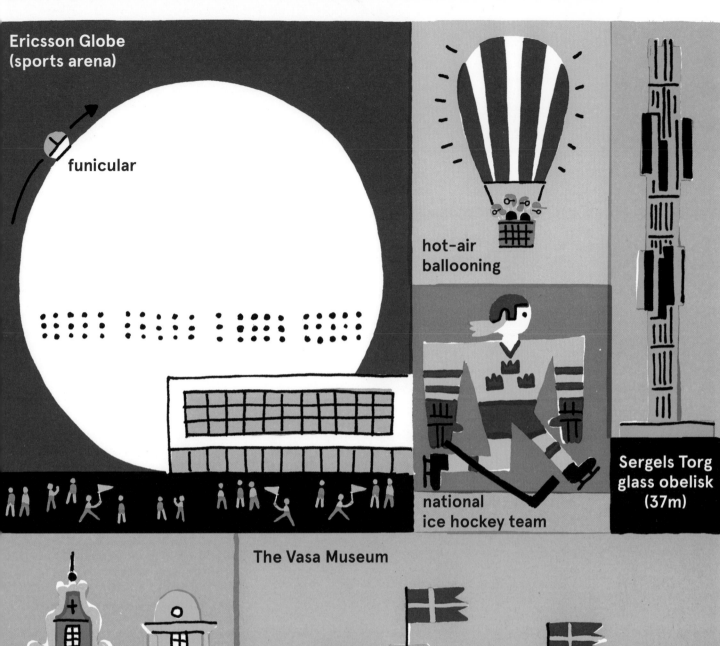

Ericsson Globe (sports arena)

funicular

hot-air ballooning

national ice hockey team

Sergels Torg glass obelisk (37m)

colourful facades on Stortorget Square

The Vasa Museum

17th-century Vasa Warship

35

MOSCOW

 14.8 million    Russian   Russia

Bolshoi Theatre

St. Basil's Cathedral

AND HOP!

ballet dancer

Spasskaya Tower

36

Kremlin

Kremlin guard

Ostankino Tower (540m)

matryoshka (Russian dolls)

Gorky Park

blinis (stuffed pancakes)

Zhivopisny Bridge

hockey player

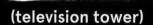
(television tower)

Metro

37

BARCELONA

👤 5 million   💬 Catalan / Spanish   🚩 Spain

sculpture

Joan Miró

football player

Sagrada Família cathedral

tapas

lizard sculpture in
Park Guell

Parc de la Ciutadella

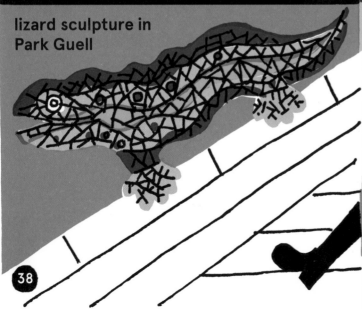

38

ROME

 4.3 million   Italian   Italy

gelato (ice cream)

OUCH!

according to legend, the Mouth of Truth bites the hand of liars

40   Italian scooter

The Coliseum

The Panthéon

traffic
policeman

Trevi Fountain

tomato and
mozzarella pizza

LET'S GO!

small Italian car

Piazza
del
Popolo

espresso
coffee

Saint Peter's
Basilica
(Vatican)

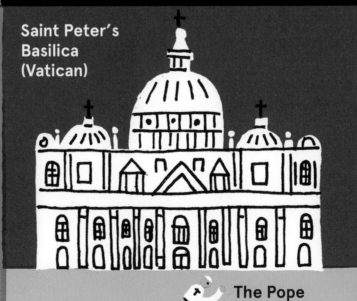

The Pope

obelisk

41

ATHENS

 3.8 million 💬 Greek 🏴 Greece

The Parthenon

KNOW THYSELF

Statue of Socrates

Acropolis of Athens

koulouri (sesame bagel)

historic area of Plaka

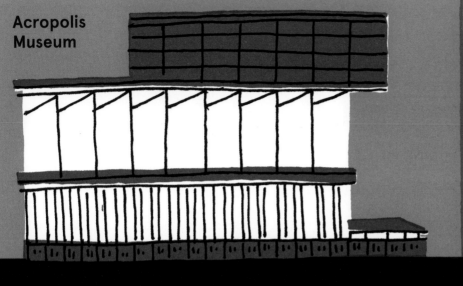

Acropolis Museum

Lycabettus Hill (277m)

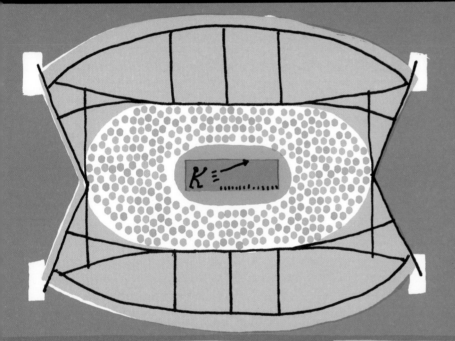

modern Olympic stadium (built in 1982)

travel by scooter

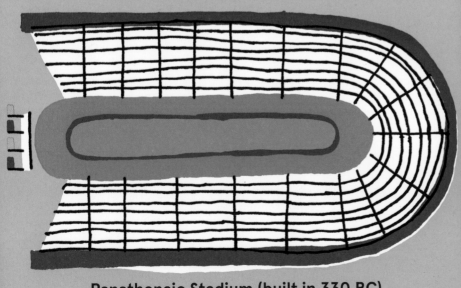

ANTIQUES! LOW PRICES!

Panathenaic Stadium (built in 330 BC)

Monastiraki Flea Market

43

ISTANBUL

👤 14.4 million   💬 Turkish   🏴 Turkey

Galata Tower (63m)

Blue Mosque

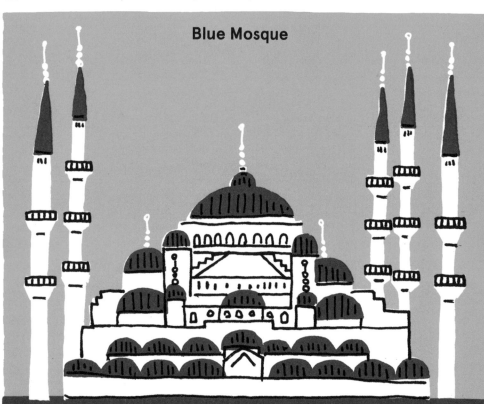

Museum of Modern Art

THIS PIECE OF ART IS MAKING ME HUNGRY!

loukoum

(Turkish delight)

Head of Medusa

Sunken Palace

FEZ

👤 1.2 mil 💬 Arabic 🏴 Morocco

couscous dish

Bab Boujloud Gate

(served with meat and vegetables)

Minaret of Medersa Bou Inania

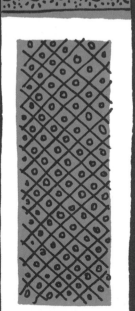

Royal Palace

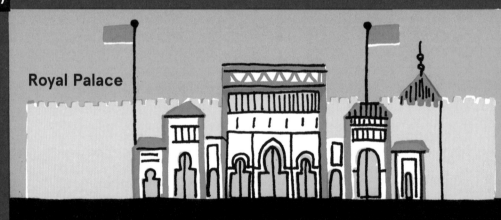

Medina of Fez (ancient walled part of the city)

traditional fountain

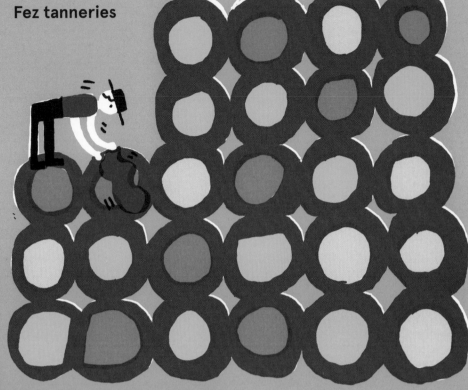

Fez tanneries

babouches (typical shoes)

at the souk (marketplace)

A PURE DELIGHT!

mint tea

Al-Qarawiyyin University

PETIT TAXI

petit taxi (small car taxicab)

47

CAIRO

👤 20.4 million   💬 Arabic (Egyptian)   🏳 Egypt

Cairo Citadel

Bab Zuwila Gate

Al-Azhar Mosque

kochari (onions, pasta, lentils and rice)

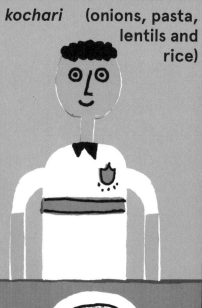

Khan el-Khalili Souk

48

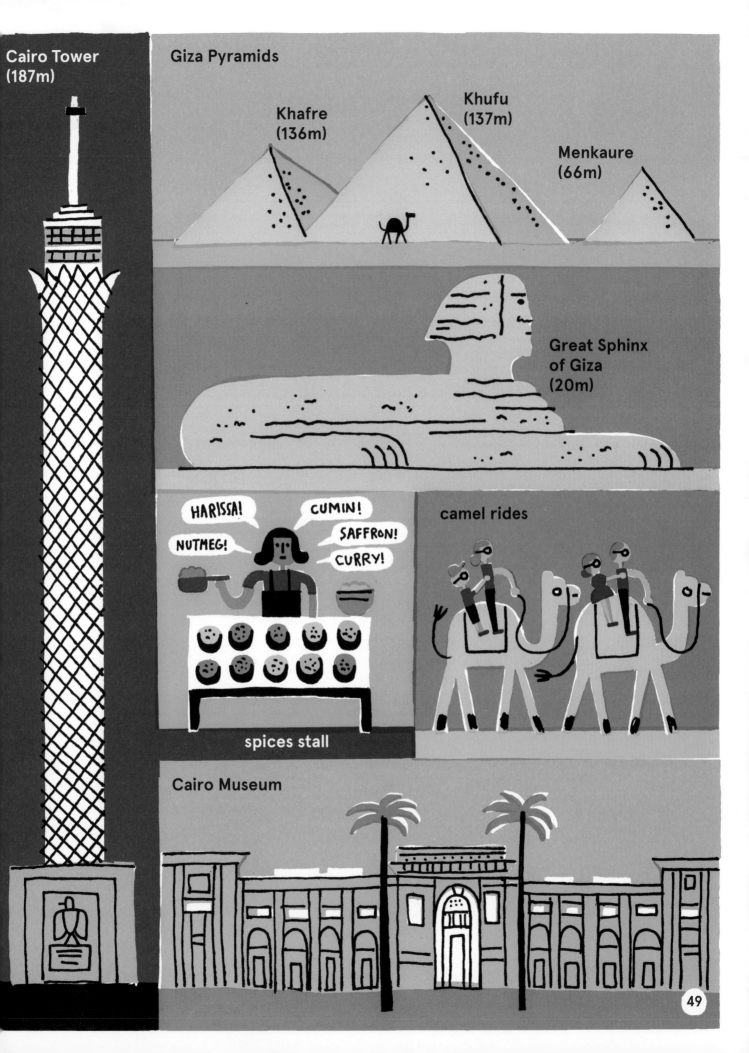

NAIROBI

👤 4.5 million   💬 English / Swahili   🏳 Kenya

Jamia Mosque

Uhuru Gardens

ride a matatu

sukuma wiki with chapati

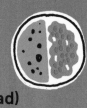

(cabbage, pancake and flatbread)

50

Kenyatta International Conference Centre (105m)

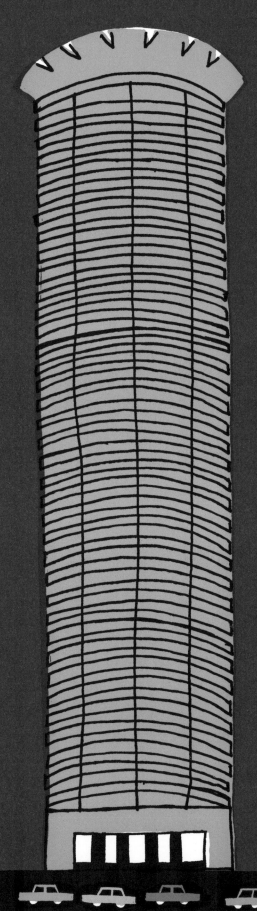

national park

Giraffe Centre

Ngong Hills wind farm

Nyayo Monument

dinosaur statue at the Nairobi National Museum

WOW!

Maasai Market

JOHANNESBURG

8 million   Nguni and Sotho languages / English / Afrikaans   South Africa

Orlando Towers in Soweto

statue of Nelson Mandela

A GREAT MAN!

rugby player

Nelson Mandela Bridge

biltong

(dried meat)

52

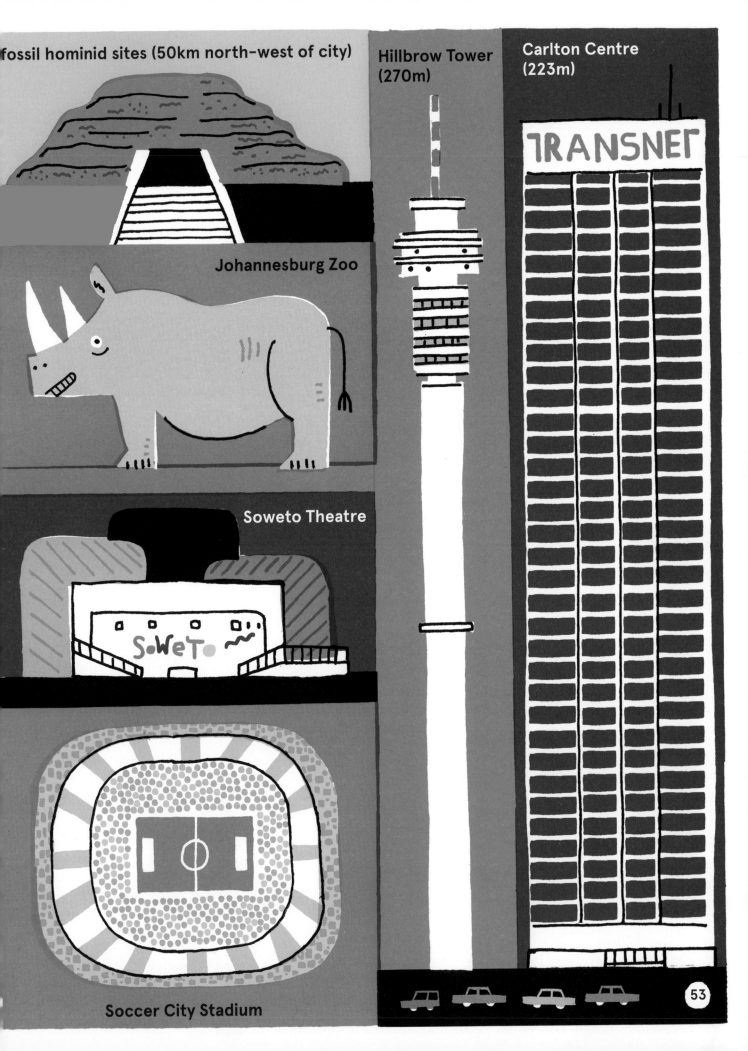

fossil hominid sites (50km north-west of city)

Johannesburg Zoo

Soweto Theatre

SOWETO

Soccer City Stadium

Hillbrow Tower (270m)

Carlton Centre (223m)

TRANSNET

53

MUMBAI

 21.9 million 💬 Marathi 🏳 India

Ganesh statue (Hindu deity)

Siddhivinayak Temple

Imperial Towers (254m)

VROOOM

rickshaw

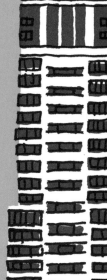

Haji Ali Dargah Mosque

Haji Ali Bay

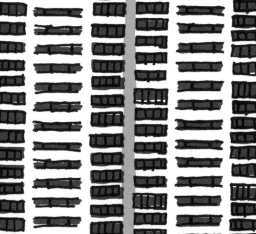

Gateway of India

dahi puri (bread stuffed with potato)

DAHI PURI

Vipassana Pagoda

corn seller on the beach

Dharavi area

WELCOME

Elephanta Caves

BANGKOK

 18.9 million 　 Thai 　 Thailand

Wat Arun
(Temple of the Dawn)

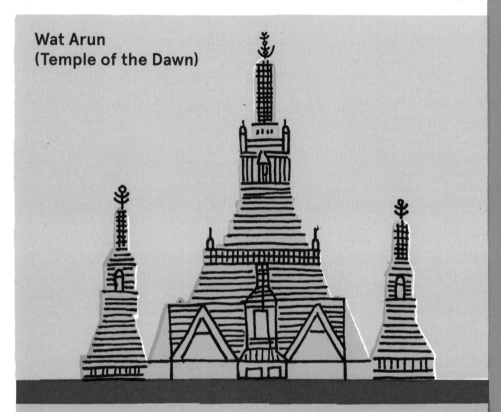

Baiyoke
Tower II
(304m)

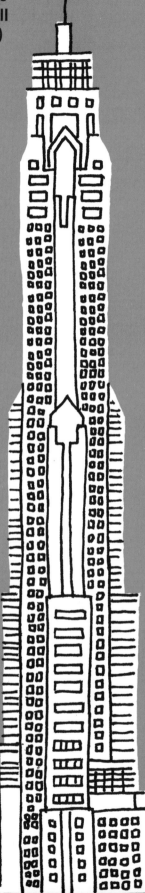

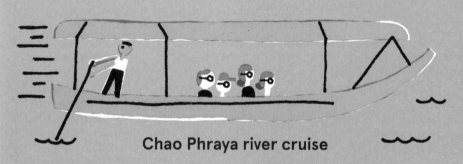

Chao Phraya river cruise

YUM!

fried beetles

56

tuk-tuk ride

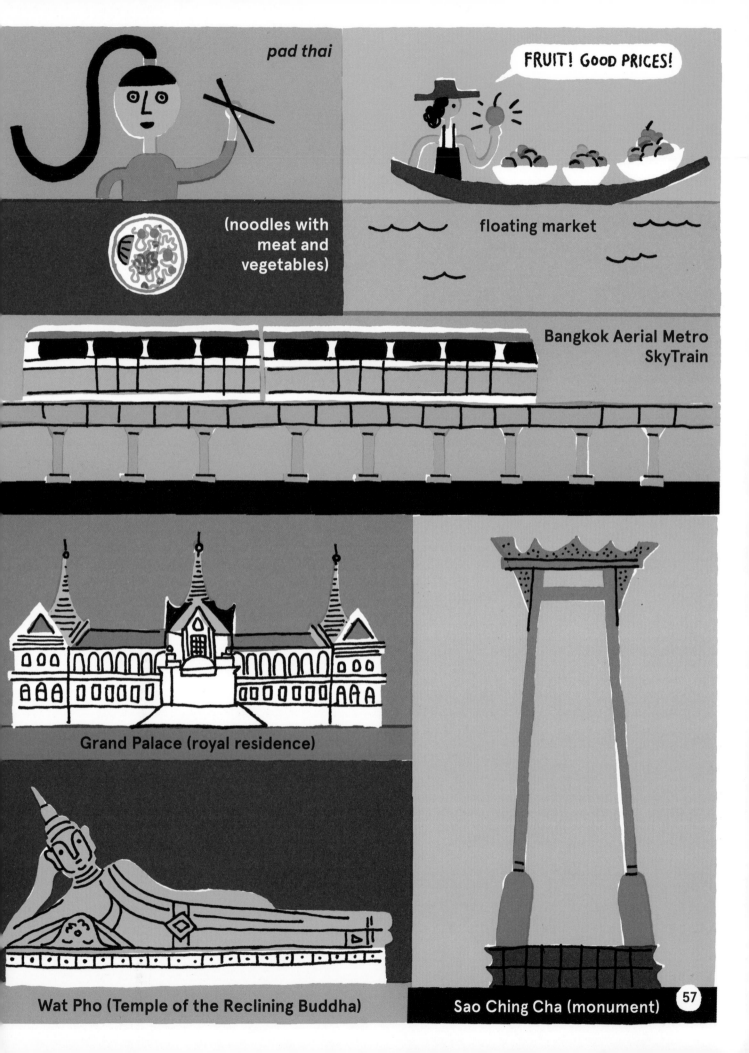

pad thai

(noodles with meat and vegetables)

FRUIT! GOOD PRICES!

floating market

Bangkok Aerial Metro SkyTrain

Grand Palace (royal residence)

Wat Pho (Temple of the Reclining Buddha)

Sao Ching Cha (monument)

HONG KONG

👤 9.6 million   💬 Cantonese / English   🏴 China

Sik Sik Yuen Wong Tai Sin Temple

Clock Tower (44m)

junk boat cruise

Star Ferry

jockey club

HERE I COME!

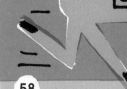

Bank of China Tower (367m)

Lin Heung Tea House

Yuen Po Bird Market

YA!

Avenue of Stars

Bruce Lee

snake soup

Peak Tower (observatory)

59

SEOUL

👤 25.6 million　💬 Korean　🏳 South Korea

Haechi statue

N Tower (237m)

Gyeongbokgung Palace

Namdaemun Market

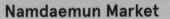

60

THIS PARK IS BEAUTIFUL!

bike ride in the Yeouido Park

Buddha statue at the Bongeunsa Temple

IFC Tower (28m)

walk along the fortress

Namsangol Hanok Teahouse

Olympic Stadium

mandu (dumpling)

National Folk Museum of Korea

TOKYO

👤 42.8 million 💬 Japanese 🏳 Japan

baseball player

Tokyo Tower (333m)

Mount Fuji (3,776m)

ramen bowl

(noodle soup)

karaoke

Shinjuku Imperial Gardens

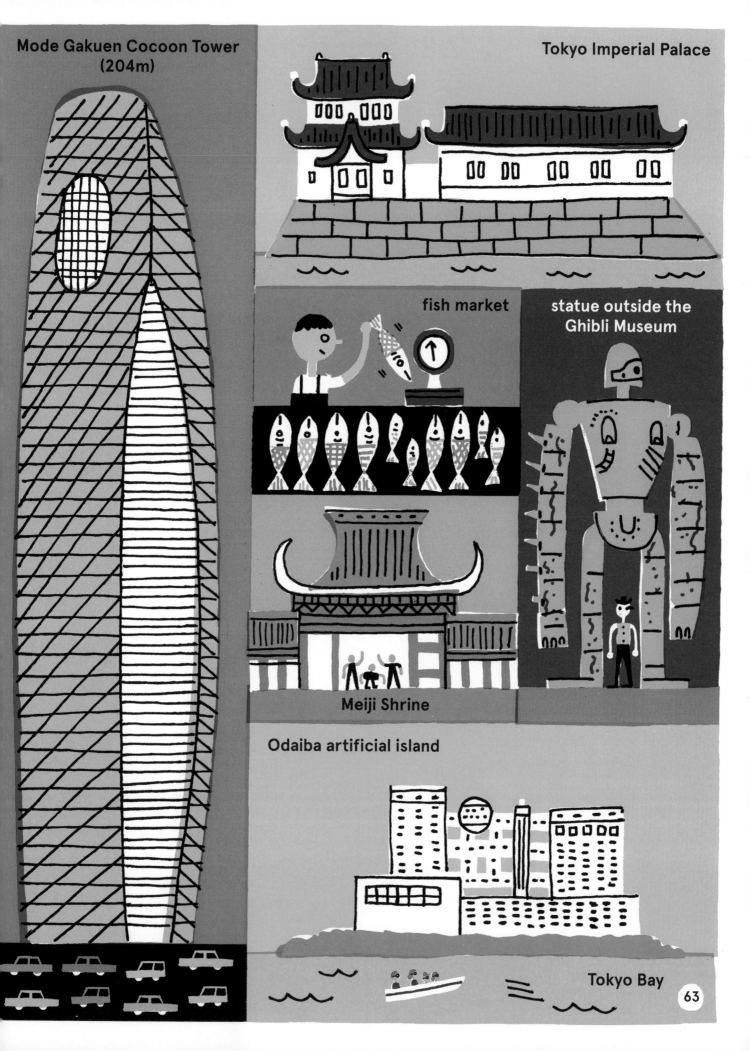

Mode Gakuen Cocoon Tower
(204m)

Tokyo Imperial Palace

fish market

statue outside the
Ghibli Museum

Meiji Shrine

Odaiba artificial island

Tokyo Bay

63

JAKARTA

 30.3 million   💬 Indonesian   🏳 Indonesia

Istiqlal Mosque

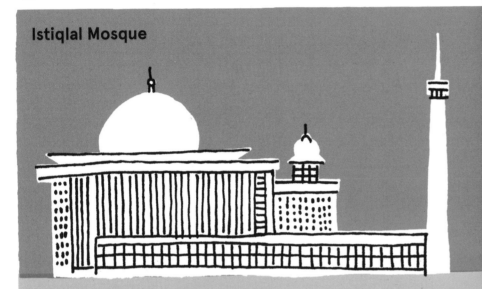

gado gado

(salad with peanut sauce)

Tamin Mini park

National Monument (137m)

Dutch drawbridge (old town area)

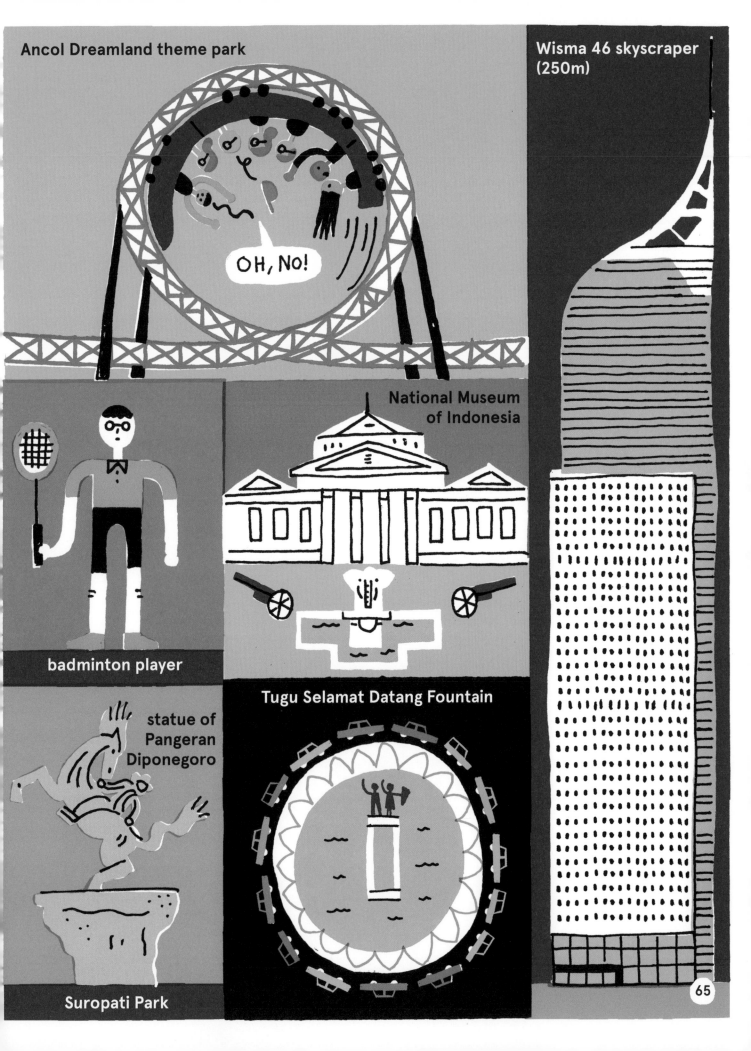

SYDNEY

👤 4.7 million   💬 English   🏳 Australia

kookaburra

(Australia's national bird)

SYDNEY IS MY FAVOURITE CITY!

Sydney Harbour Bridge

Sydney Opera House

Sydney Harbour

harbour cruise

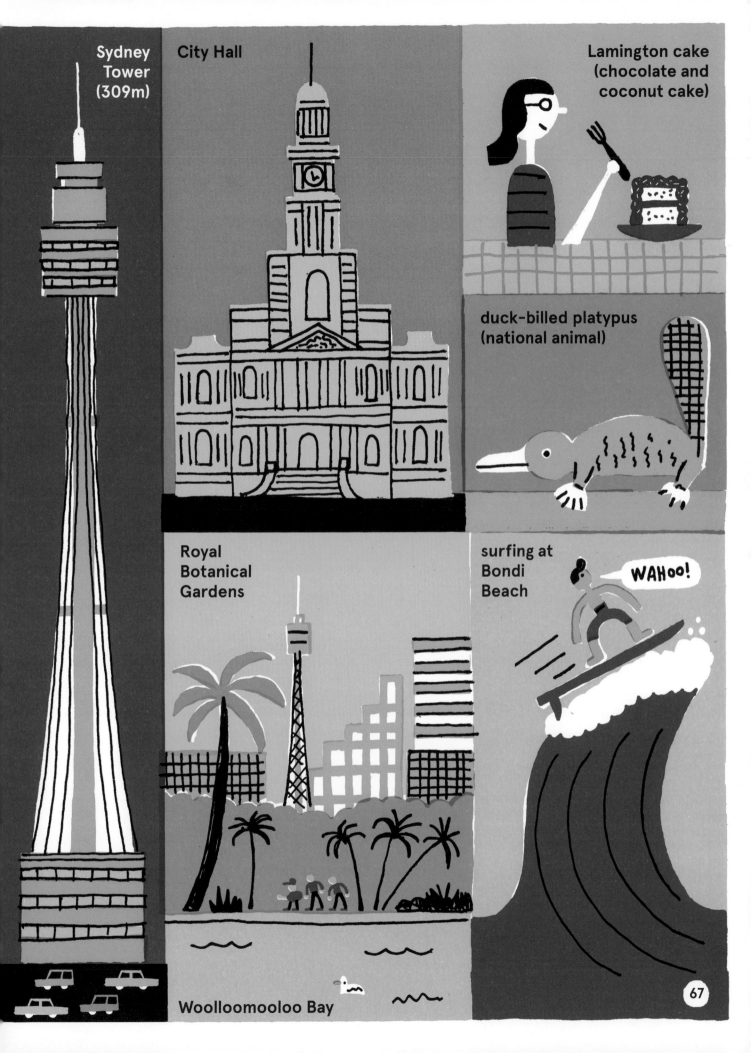

Sydney Tower (309m)

City Hall

Lamington cake (chocolate and coconut cake)

duck-billed platypus (national animal)

Royal Botanical Gardens

surfing at Bondi Beach

WAHOO!

Woolloomooloo Bay

AUCKLAND

 1.4 million  English New Zealand

Auckland War Memorial Museum

DELICIOUS!

pavlova (meringue, whipped cream and fruit)

Tamaki Maori Village

Auckland Harbour Bridge

Sante-Marie Bay

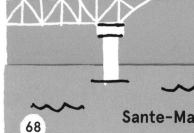

Sky Tower (328m)